To All Children

Copyright © 2023 by Zeinab Shalaby.

All Rights Reserved. No part of this book may be reproduced, transmitted, or stored in an information retrieval system in any form or by any means, graphic, electronic, or mechanical, including photocopying, taping, and recording, without prior written permission from the publisher.

Edited by Wafaa Shalaby and Noha Elmouelhi

First edition 2023

ISBN 978-1-959536-04-8

Published by Honey Elm Books LLC
www.HoneyElmBooks.com

MUHAMMAD:
The Seal of the Prophets

Written and Illustrated by:

Zeinab Shalaby

Prophet Muhammad (pbuh) was born in Mecca in what we know now as Saudi Arabia in Asia. He was born almost 600 years after Jesus (pbuh). At that time, people in Arabia lived in tribes. Muhammad's family was from a noble tribe named Qureish. Muhammad's father (Abdullah) died before he was born. His mother (Aminah) took care of him with love and tenderness. Sadly, Aminah passed away while Muhammad was just 6 years old.

Muhammad (pbuh) had a big loving family. His grandfather (Abd Elmottaleb) took care of him afterward. Then, Muhammad's uncle (Abou Talib) took over and raised him with all his kids. This orphan boy had very noble character. He was very honest and trustworthy. Later on, Muhammad (pbuh) began to travel with the caravans that traveled north and returned with many goods back to Mecca.

At age 25, Muhammad (pbuh) married Khadija bint Khowaylad. She was the best wife and the best mother to their four daughters: Zeinab, Ruqayya, Om Kolthoum and Fatima. Later on, Muhammad (pbuh) took care of his younger cousin (Aly Ibn Abi Talib). Aly was close to Muhammad (pbuh) and looked up to him. Aly will play a very important role later in his life.

When Muhammad (pbuh) was growing up, people in Arabia worshipped idols. They forgot what Abraham and Ishmael (pbut) had taught them about worshipping the One and True God (Allah The Almighty). They had idols inside and all around the Kaabah. Their beliefs were full of superstitions and false practices.

Did Muhammad believe in idol worshipping?

Muhammad never believed in idol worshipping. He did not follow any of their false practices either.

The Arabs were known for many noble traits like bravery, integrity, hospitality and honoring their word. They excelled in the Arabic language and poetry. Muhammad (pbuh) did not know how to read or write, but he was known for his truthfulness and sound judgment.

Muhammad (pbuh) took care of his family and had a great relationship with the people around him. But he could not understand why his people worshipped man-made statues. Muhammad (pbuh) did not follow their ignorant practices. He started to spend the month of Ramadan every year in a cave at the outskirts of Mecca, meditating and wondering about the creation of the universe. This cave is known as the Cave of Hiraa.

One night while Muhammad (pbuh) was in the cave of Hiraa, Angel Jibril (pbuh) appeared to him and held him tightly, commanding him to READ. Muhammad (pbuh) was perplexed and answered: I cannot read. But Jibril (pbuh) insisted and repeated the same command several times. Hesitant and afraid, Muhammad (pbuh) asked: What should I read? Finally, Jibril (pbuh) revealed the first words of the Holy Quran: "Read in the Name of your Lord, Who has created (all that exists)."

"Read in the Name of your Lord, Who has created (all that exists)"

"اَقْرَأْ بِٱسْمِ رَبِّكَ ٱلَّذِى خَلَقَ"

Al-Alaq: 1 (العلق)

God is One

لا إله إلا الله

Muhammad (pbuh) was shaken by what had happened in the cave. He rushed home and asked his wife to cover him with whatever blankets she might have. He told Khadija the whole story of the events at the cave. He was afraid that he might be sick. She comforted him and told him that she believed that God had chosen him to be the next messenger to mankind. She truly believed in her husband's noble character. Khadija (May Allah be pleased with her) was the first person to embrace Islam and support Muhammad in his new mission. Muhammad (pbuh) was 40 years old when he received the first revelation of the Quran.

Soon after, Allah (The Almighty) commanded Muhammad to invite people to worship the One and True God and to abolish idol worshipping. He did exactly that. At the beginning, he invited people around him secretly. Some people answered his call immediately like his close friend Abou Bakr Alsiddiq. Even his young cousin, Aly Ibn Abi Talib, submitted to Islam right away.

Unfortunately, new Muslims could not practice their religion in public. Prophet Muhammad (pbuh) used to meet secretly with the new Muslims at a home called The House of Al Arqam. There, Prophet Muhammad (pbuh) used to teach them their religion away from the eyes of Qureish.

God is One

لا إله إلا الله

Three years later, Prophet Muhammad (pbuh) started to publicly invite all Meccans to Islam. More people answered his call. But the leaders of Qureish refused to submit to this new message. They did everything they could to stop this new religion. They tortured new Muslims whenever they could. They even tried to stop Muhammad (pbuh) by all means but they failed.

The people of Qureish never gave up. They harassed Muslims and even besieged them. Qureish imposed a huge economic embargo against Muslims for almost three years. But the Muslims were strong in their faith and tolerated all that with patience and perseverance.

After the embargo was lifted, Muhammad (pbuh) lost two of his most beloved and supportive people in his life. Both his uncle (Abou Talib) and his wife (Khadija) passed away. For this reason, that year was called "the year of sorrow."

After the death of Abou Talib, Qureish intensified their animosity against Muhammad (pbuh) and the Muslims.

During that tough period, Allah (The Exalted) rewarded Muhammad (pbuh) with a spiritual journey to Jerusalem. This is called "Esraa". Then Muhammad (pbuh) ascended to different levels of heaven. This is called "Miraj". This journey of Esraa and Miraj gave Muhammad (pbuh) peace and comfort. The five daily prayers were also prescribed for Muslims during this journey.

Islam started to spread in and around Mecca. Among the places where Islam was spreading was a city north of Mecca. This city was called Yathrib.

When it became too difficult for Muslims to practice their religion in Mecca, Prophet Muhammad (pbuh) advised them to migrate to Yathrib. They did and were welcomed by the people of Yathrib. This was 13 years after Muhammad (pbuh) received the first revelation of the Quran.

When Qureish discovered that the Muslims were migrating to Yathrib, they were furious. They feared that the Muslims would become stronger and that other people would follow them. This would mean an end to the power of Qureish.

The leaders of Qureish decided to get rid of Muhammad (pbuh) himself to put an end to his message. They decided to choose one person from each family and to have them all kill Muhammad at the same time. They planned to carry out their plot at dawn.

When prophet Muhammad (pbuh) found out about this plot, he decided to migrate to Yathrib with his close friend Abou Bakr. They left at night and his young cousin, Aly Ibn Abi Talib, slept in the prophet's bed to trick the people of Qureish while Muhammad and Abou Bakr started on their way to Yathrib.

At dawn, the Qureishi rushed to the prophet's house to carry out their plot. To their surprise, Muhammad was not there. Having no interest in Aly, they left fuming and disappointed.

Prophet Muhammad (pbuh) and Abou Bakr started their journey of migration to Yathrib. They were followed by the people of Qureish. The Prophet and Abou Bakr decided to hide in a cave called Cave of Thowr. and stayed there for three nights. The Qureishi came so close to their cave that Abou Bakr was so worried that they might find them. Prophet Muhammad comforted him and told him that he was sure that God (The Almighty) would save them. When the people of Qureish came across the cave, they found a spider web at the cave's entrance. They thought that the cave must have been deserted a long time ago. They left and God saved prophet Muhammad (pbuh) and Abou Bakr. When it was safe, prophet Muhammad (pbuh) and Abou Bakr continued their journey to Yathrib.

The people of Yathrib welcomed them and were racing to help them and all the Muslims who migrated from Mecca. There was a sense of joy and happiness throughout the city.

This wonderful city became known as Medina. This new name means "The City" in reference to the city of The Prophet (pbuh).

In Medina, the Muslims started to feel safe and to have a community. They built the first mosque in Medina. It was their place of worship and gathering. This event of migration marked the beginning of the Muslim Calendar (Hijri Calendar).

Do you know the months of the Muslim calendar?

When the Muslims migrated from Mecca to Medina, they left their homes and belongings behind. Prophet Muhammad (pbuh) encouraged the Muslims of Medina to help the Muslims of Mecca and to treat them as their sisters and brothers. And they did. Since then, the Muslims of Mecca were known as The Migrants "Almuhajireen" and the Muslims of Medina were known as The Helpers "Alansar". Together they built a wonderful community.

Will Qureish leave the Muslims alone in their new home?

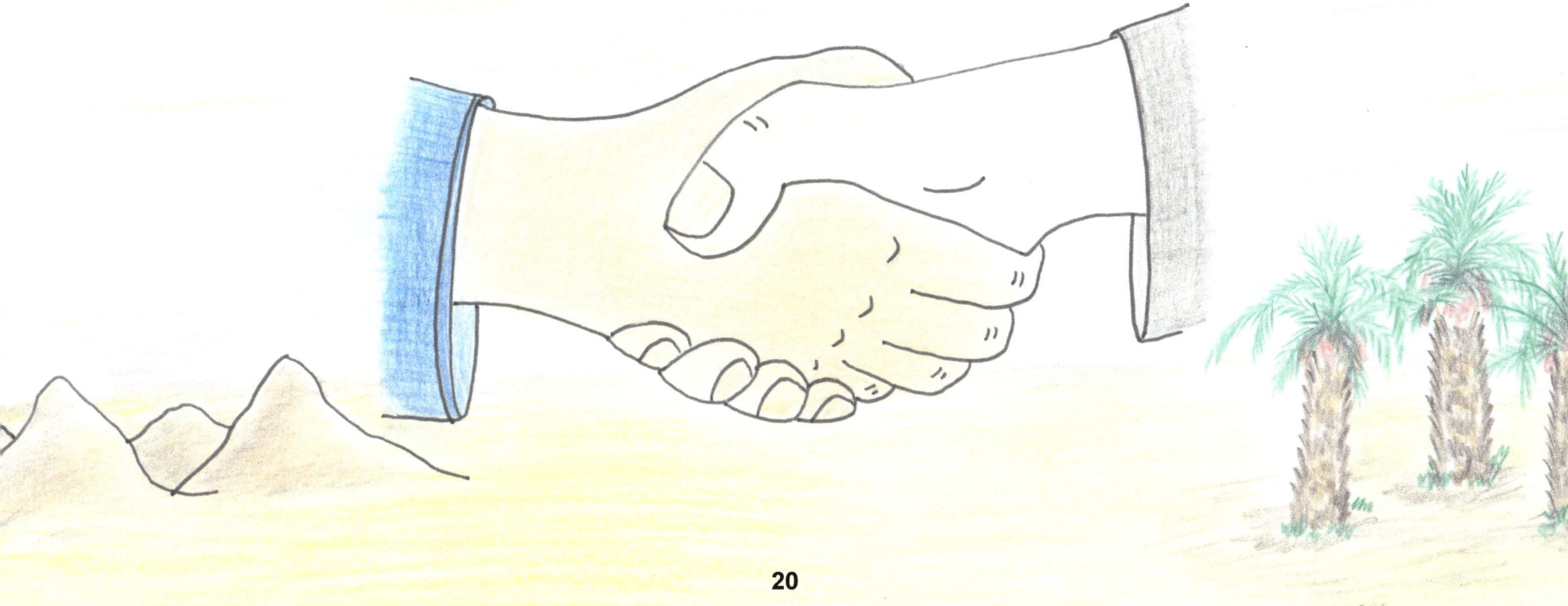

The leaders of Qureish never gave up. They kept plotting against the Muslims and fighting them even after the Muslims had left Mecca. Years passed and finally Qureish surrendered. A peaceful agreement was reached between the Muslims and Qureish. The Muslims conquered Mecca on the eighth year after Hijra. Prophet Muhammad (pbuh) destroyed all the idols inside and around the Kabaa. He treated all the people of Mecca with dignity and forgave his past enemies. Many of them accepted Islam and became good Muslims.

Two years later, Prophet Muhammad (pbuh) led the Muslims in a journey of Hajj to Mecca.

During this Hajj, Prophet Muhammad (pbuh) gave a farewell speech. He encouraged all Muslims to adhere to the guidance of Allah (The Almighty) and to help each other. He emphasized the principles of Islam. Prophet Muhammad (pbuh) announced that he had completed his mission and delivered the true religion of Islam.

A few months later, Prophet Muhammad (pbuh) passed away after a short illness and was buried in Medina. He left behind a very strong Muslim community that would carry his message beyond Arabia. Muslims would build the most prosperous civilization. A civilization that was based on the principles of Islam of piety, peace, liberty, equality and justice for all. A message that was delivered by Prophet Muhammad (pbuh) – the Seal of the Prophets.

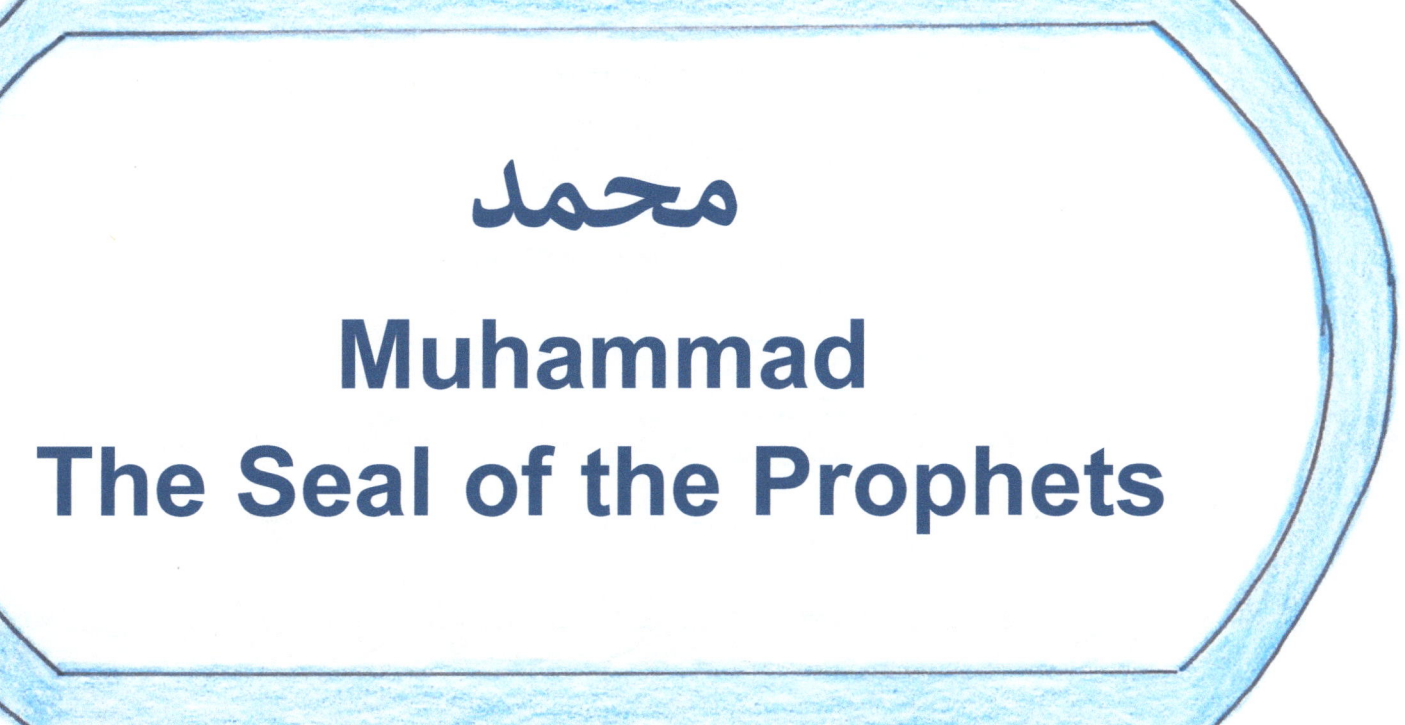

محمد

**Muhammad
The Seal of the Prophets**

Did you know that the names in this story can be read in either English or Arabic?

English Name	Arabic Name	الإسم العربي
God	Allah	الله
Muhammad	Muhammad	محمد
Abou Talib	Abou Talib	أبو طالب
Khadija	Khadija	خديجة
Abou Bakr	Abou Bakr	أبو بكر
Aly	Aly	علي
Qureish	Qureish	قريش
Almuhajireen	Almuhajireen	المهاجرين
Alansar	Alansar	الأنصار
Hijra	Hijra	هجرة
Mecca	Makkah	مكة
Medina	Madinah	مدينة

www.ingramcontent.com/pod-product-compliance
Lightning Source LLC
Chambersburg PA
CBHW050848010526
44107CB00017BA/1219